Visiting the Vet

words by Robyn Opie
photographs by Russell Millard

A vet is an animal doctor. Vets help animals when they are sick or hurt.

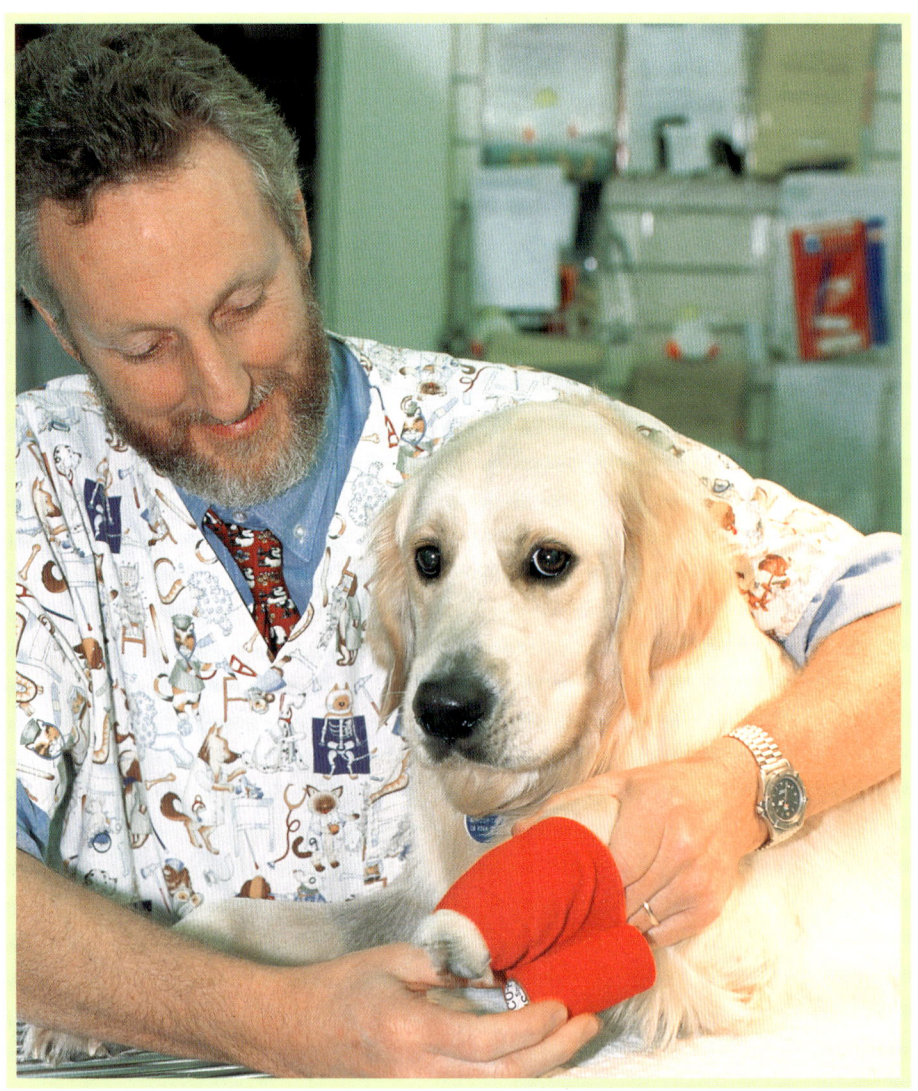

A vet also helps to stop animals from getting sick. This dog is visiting a vet for a checkup.

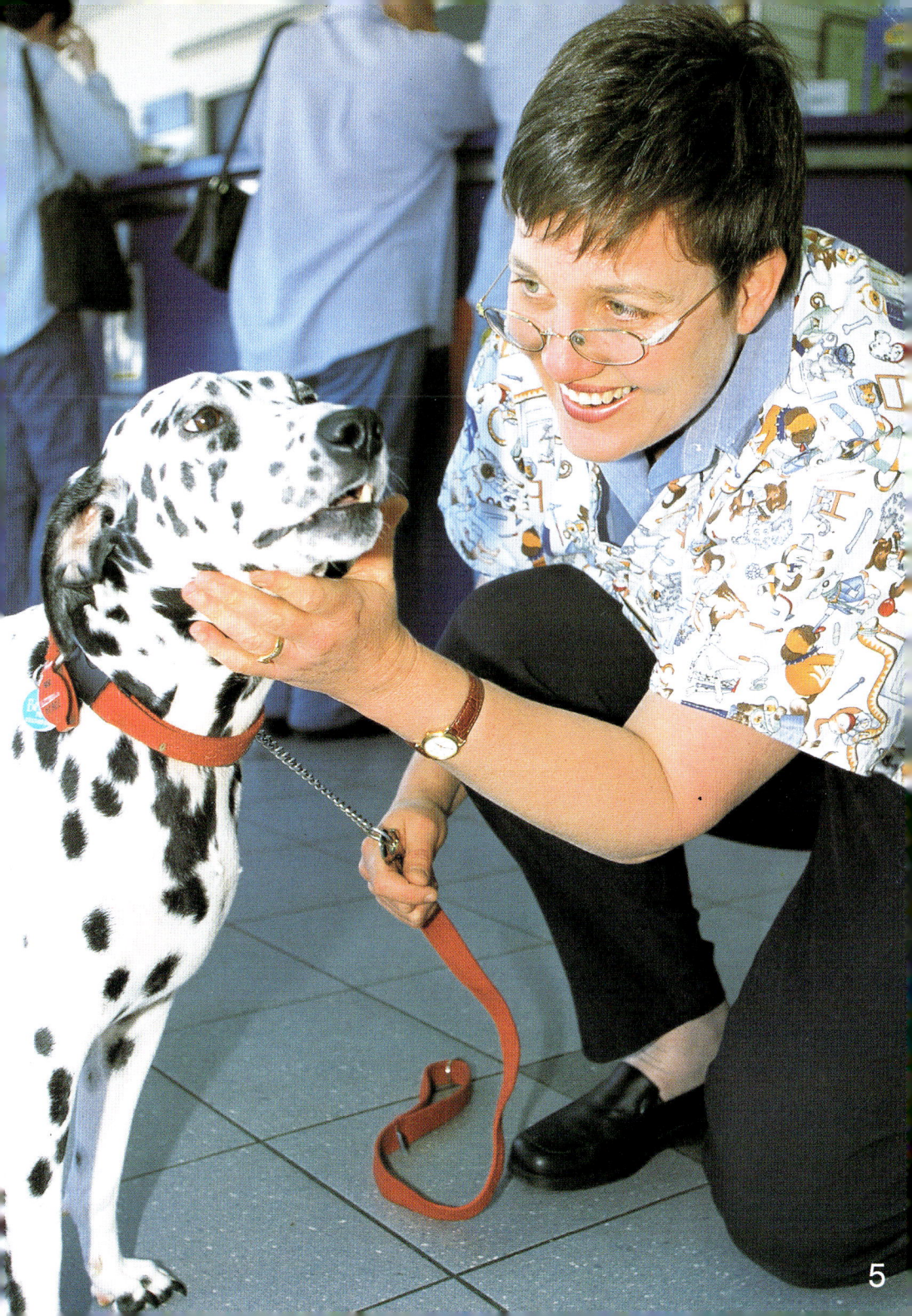

The vet looks at the dog's teeth and gums. They tell the vet a lot about how well the dog is.

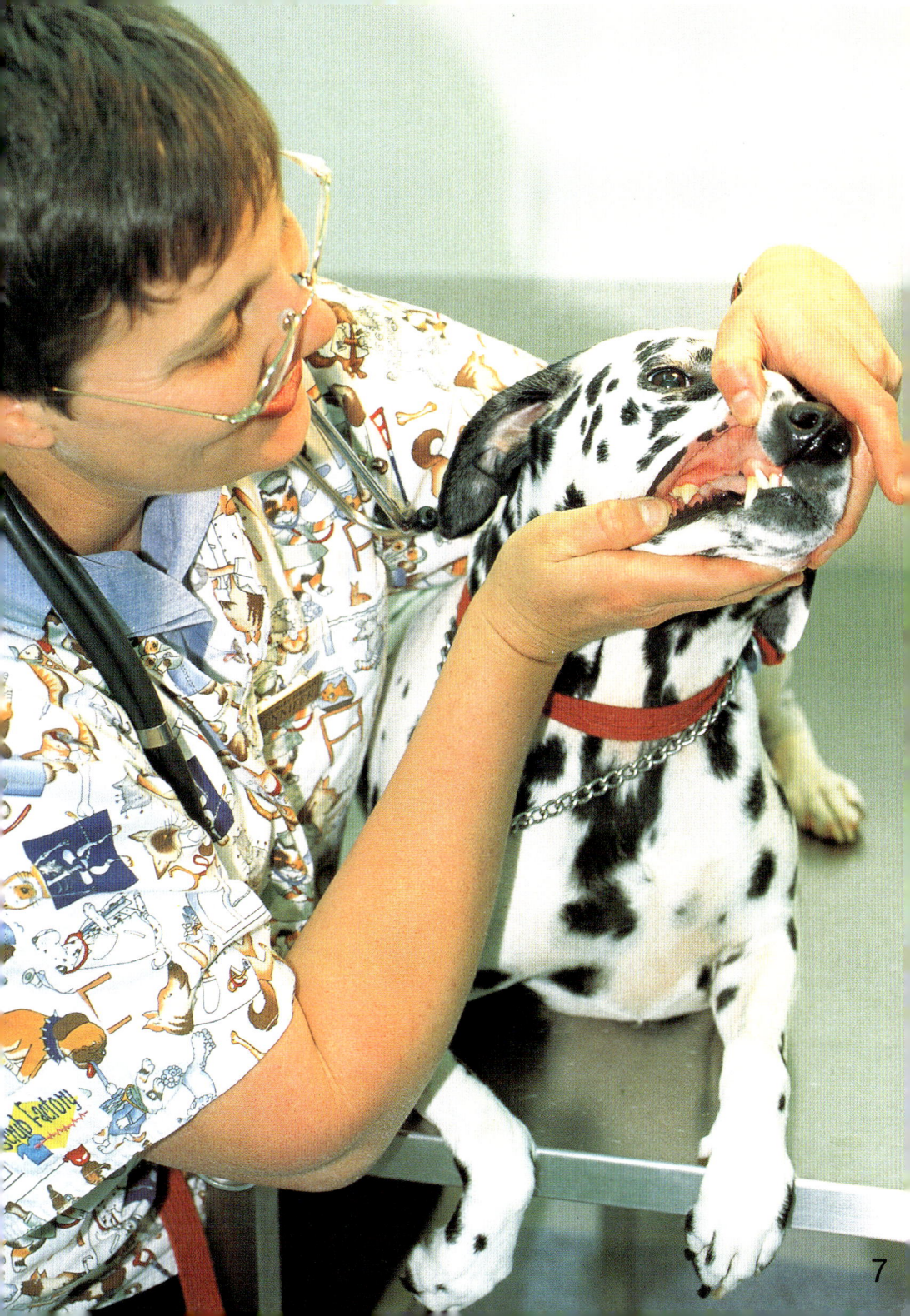

The vet uses a small light to look in the dog's ears.

She weighs the dog on the big scales.

The vet uses a needle to give the dog medicine. It will stop the dog from catching other dogs' germs.

The vet gives the dog pills. They stop the dog from getting worms.

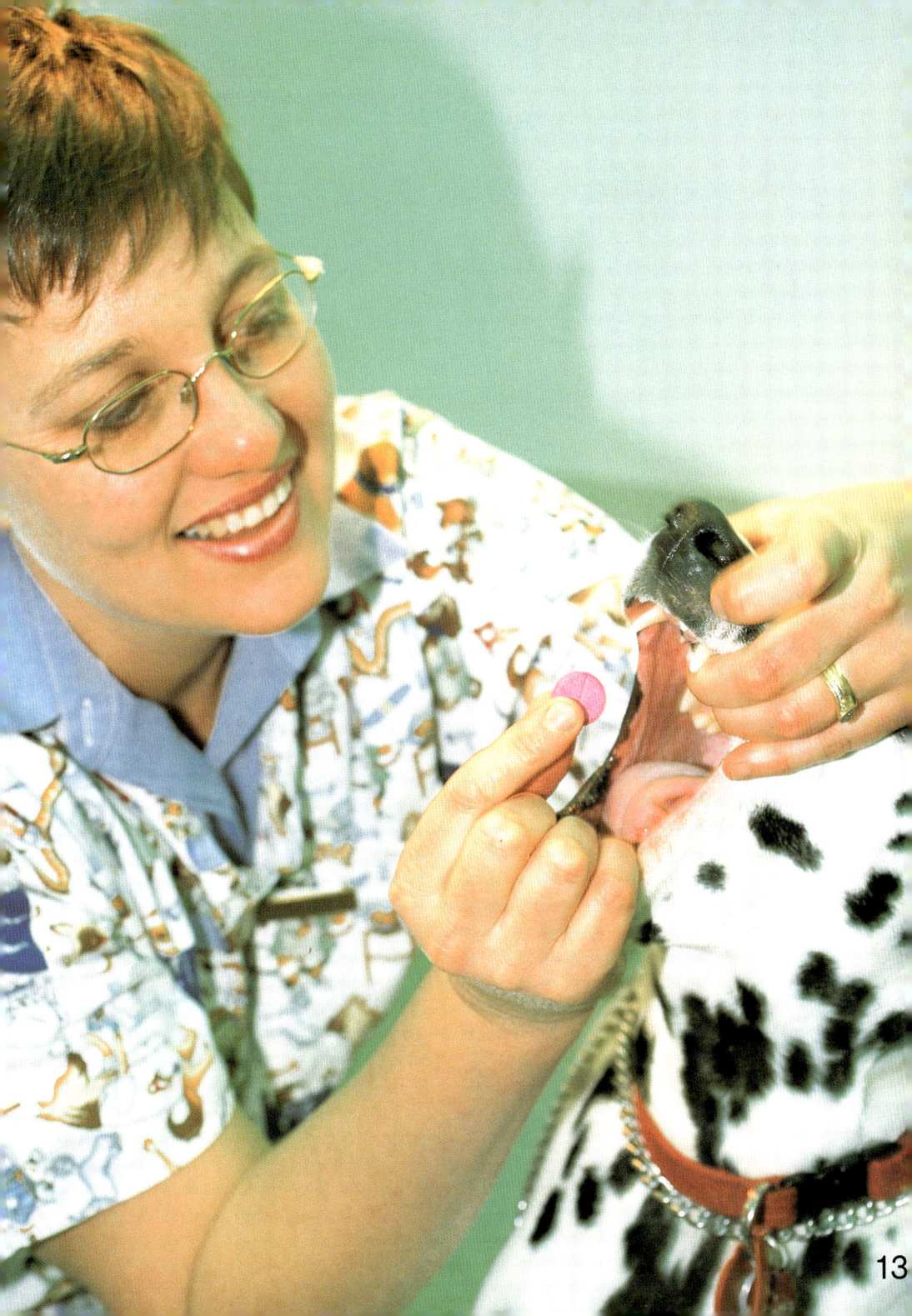

The checkup is over, and it's time to go home.

The vet gives the dog a treat because she has been very good…

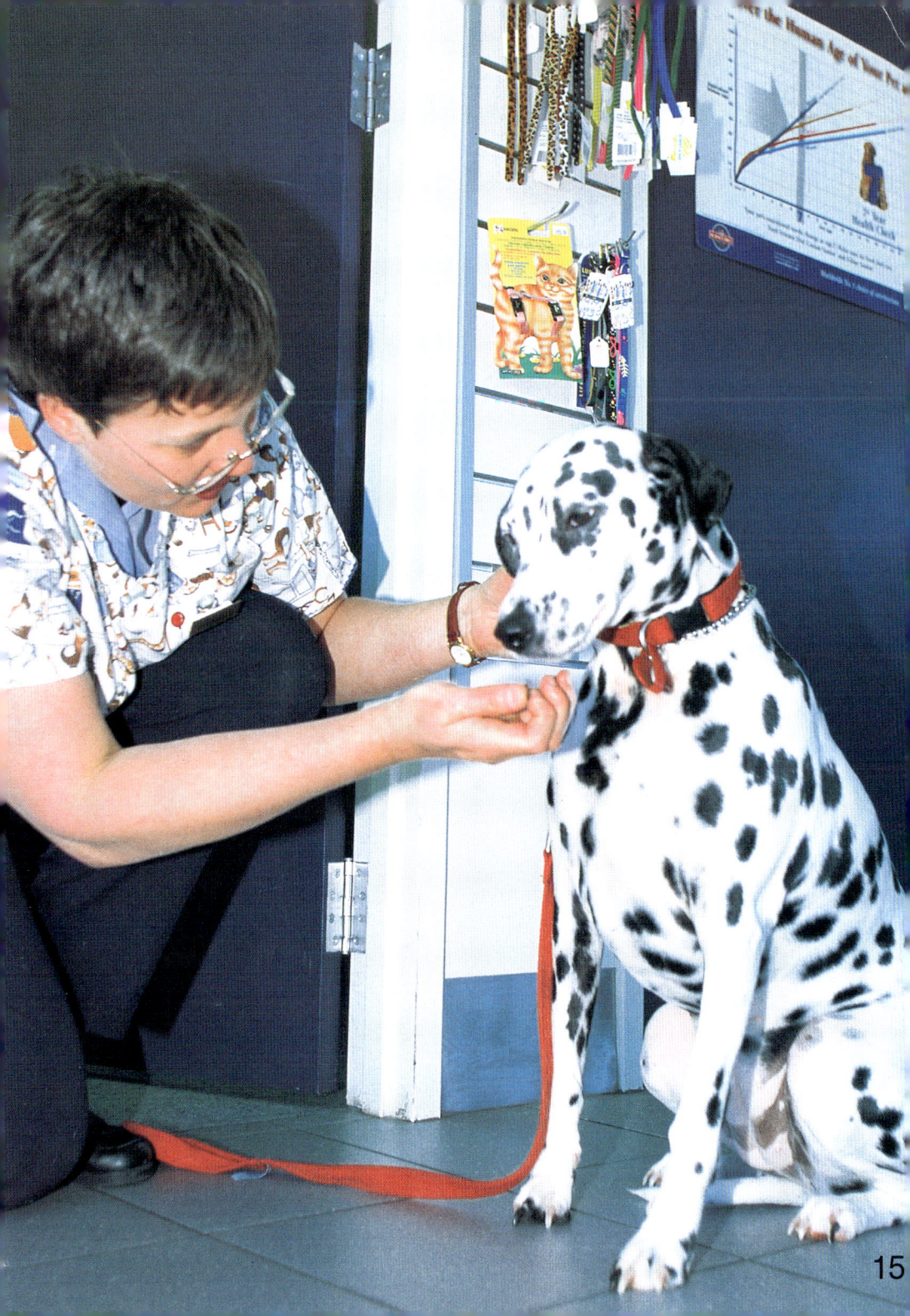

until she sees a cat in the waiting room.